J
310

DATE DUE

AUG 3 0 2008	

DEMCO, INC. 38-2931

Today's Superstars
Entertainment

Kenny Chesney

by William David Thomas

Gareth Stevens
Publishing

Please visit our web site at: www.garethstevens.com
For a free color catalog describing Gareth Stevens Publishing's
list of high-quality books, call 1-800-542-2595 (USA) or
1-800-387-3178 (Canada).

Library of Congress Cataloging-in-Publication Data

Thomas, William, 1947-
     Kenny Chesney / by William David Thomas.
          p. cm. — (Today's superstars. Entertainment)
     Includes bibliographical references and index.
     ISBN: 978-0-8368-8198-1 (lib. bdg.)
     1. Chesney, Kenny. 2. Country musicians—United States—
Biography. I. Title.
ML420.C4722T56   2008
782.421642092—dc22
     [B]   2007002998

This edition first published in 2008 by
Gareth Stevens Publishing
A Weekly Reader® Company
1 Reader's Digest Road
Pleasantville, NY 10570-7000 USA

Copyright © 2008 by Gareth Stevens, Inc.

Editor: Gini Holland
Art direction and design: Tammy West
Picture research: Diane Laska-Swanke
Production: Jessica Yanke

Photo credits: Cover, pp. 5, 15, 19, 23, 28 © AP Images; p. 6 © Evan
Yee/LADN/WireImage.com; p. 9 © East Tennessee State University; p. 11
© Philip Gould/CORBIS; p. 13 © Tim Mosenfelder/Getty Images; p. 17
© Fotos International/Getty Images; p. 20 © Tim Mosenfelder/CORBIS;
p. 22 © George Taylor/Everett Collection; p. 25 © TriStar/courtesy Everett
Collection; p. 26 © Rusty Russell/Getty Images

Printed in the United States of America

1 2 3 4 5 6 7 8 9 11 10 09 08 07

Contents

Chapter 1

Connecting

What kind of a concert was this? When Kenny Chesney plays and sings, thousands of people show up. This audience had fewer than one hundred people. Kenny's fans wear jeans, boots, and cowboy hats. At this show, the women wore long dresses. The men wore tuxedos and polished black shoes. When Kenny sings, his fans often sing along. When a song ends, they shout and cheer. This crowd listened, and then clapped politely.

It was May 16, 2006. The concert took place at the White House in Washington, D.C. Kenny was invited there by the president of the United States, George

W. Bush. The people in the audience were U.S. senators and representatives, foreign leaders, and special guests.

Kenny's songs were not the kind of music some of these people were used to hearing. Everyone in the audience felt something, however. They understood the stories and feelings in Kenny's music. They felt, in some way, connected to him.

For Kenny Chesney, connecting with people is what it's all about. It is really

Kenny — wearing a black cowboy hat — sings in the East Room of the White House in 2006. President George W. Bush and Mrs. Bush are in the front row, on the right side.

important to him. It is what keeps him singing, writing, and traveling. He says, "It's one thing to have a hit song, but another to have people connect with you. That's really special."

When people are waiting to get into his concerts, Kenny often goes out and talks to them. He walks up and down the lines, shaking hands and signing autographs. People feel like they know him. Once the music starts, they really feel it. Kenny says, "I grew up in a very small town. . . . I got

Fact File

For a long time, Kenny tried to keep his middle name a secret. It finally got out. His full name is Kenneth Arnold Chesney.

to play football. . . . I fished in a lake, had my heart broken. . . . And I think that's why people buy my records. . . . They feel like the songs are about their lives. . . . I'm not all that different from them, even now."

Kenny is now rich and famous, but he still behaves like a guy from a small town. He knows what is important to him. He always remembers his family, his friends, and the people who helped him along the way. That is said about a lot of stars. In Kenny's case, it is true.

When he was invited to play that concert at the White House, Kenny was told he could bring only one guest. This man is a country music superstar. His albums sell millions of copies. He's received the highest awards in country music. So who was his date for this special event? Kenny brought his mom.

Fact File

Kenny still has a T-shirt that belonged to his high school girlfriend.

7

Chapter 2

Where I'm From

"I love it back home," Kenny says. "I love where I'm from. I love being from a place where everybody knows everybody." That place is a little town called Luttrell, in the eastern part of Tennessee.

Kenny was born on March 26, 1968. His parents, David and Karen Chesney, divorced when he was very young. He still grew up surrounded by family. Kenny and his younger sister, Jennifer, spent a lot of time with grandparents, aunts, uncles, and cousins.

Kenny's mom, Karen, worked as a hair stylist. She didn't earn much money. Kenny remembers playing baseball with rocks he picked up from his driveway. He'd hit them using a broom handle for

a bat. He was serious about sports. He says, "I loved school. . . . I liked class and all, but really, when you're a young guy in East Tennessee, it's all about football and sports."

Kenny was determined to play on his high school football team. He was small — Kenny is only 5 feet, 6 inches (168 centimeters) tall — but he became a starter on the team. He once said he was probably the smallest, slowest receiver in the history of high school football.

He learned an important lesson playing football. "I learned that it wasn't OK just to be

This is part of the campus at East Tennessee State University. Kenny graduated in 1991.

Fact File

Kenny's sister Jennifer always calls him "Buh." That's short for Bubba. One younger cousin always calls him "Ninny."

good," Kenny says. "That's where I learned to go the extra mile, to work really hard to achieve something." It was a lesson he would later apply to his music career.

Things Begin To Change

Kenny graduated from Gibbs High School in 1987. That fall he started college at East Tennessee State University. He came home at Christmas time. He wanted to see his family and eat some of his grandma's chocolate pie. He got a special Christmas present that year. It was a brand new guitar.

Kenny took his guitar back to college and practiced. When he started singing and playing, people began paying attention to him. He wasn't really popular at college, he says, "until I put a guitar on my shoulder. Then it all kind of changed just a little bit."

It didn't change just a little bit. It changed a whole lot.

Fact File

Not far from Kenny's home town of Luttrell is another small town. Its name is Chesney, Tennessee.

Chet Atkins

Luttrell, Tennessee, is also the home town of country music star Chet Atkins. Atkins was famous for his guitar playing. He helped create the Nashville Sound. This was a style that mixed country music with pop music. Chet Atkins won eleven Grammy Awards in his career. He died of cancer in 2001.

The great guitarist and country music legend Chet Atkins performs in 1976.

Chapter 3

On His Way

The guitar he got for Christmas changed Kenny. He decided what he wanted to do with his life. He says, "I made up my mind I was going to figure out how to make my living playing music." He worked very hard at music. He was going to college full time. He was taking classes and doing assignments. But he was also practicing his music. Sometimes he worked on music for seven hours a day.

Kenny joined a campus bluegrass band. Later he started playing at a place in Johnson City, near the college. It was called Chucky's Trading Post. Kenny played there five nights a week. He played songs made famous by other

Kenny started wearing cowboy hats early in his career. They are always black or white. Here, in 1996, he's singing in California.

country singers, such as George Jones and Hank Williams Jr. He earned very little money, but he was gaining experience.

Music Burned Inside Me

Soon Kenny began to write his own songs. He sang them in places around Johnson City, then at places farther away. "I got to where I had a pretty good following," he says. It was hard being a student and a musician at the same time. Kenny remembers long hours and not much sleep.

The Grigsby Twins

Kenny's mom, Karen, has a twin sister named Sharon. When they were young, the sisters sang gospel music together. They were known as the Grigsby Twins. Kenny's grandfather was their "roadie." A "roadie" is someone who helps the band when they are on the road. He drove the girls all over East Tennessee while they sang at churches, fairs, and theaters.

He tells how he would rent sound gear from a store in Johnson City. He would load it into his truck and drive places where he was playing. Sometimes he would sing and play until two o'clock in the morning. Then he would drive back to Johnson City and sleep in the truck until the music store opened. He would return the sound gear, get something to eat, and then go to class. It was really hard. Kenny says, "That's how music burned inside me." He means that he really, really wanted to make music. He wanted it so much that he would do almost anything so he could sing and play.

Kenny and some friends recorded an album of songs he had written. He paid

to have a thousand copies of the album made. He began selling them wherever he played. Kenny used the money from his album sales to buy a Martin guitar.

He graduated from college in 1991. Kenny's degree was in **marketing** and advertising. That wasn't the work he wanted to do, however. He wanted to make music. He says, "I would have been a very bad advertising salesman, and I would have been very unhappy." Kenny moved to Nashville, Tennessee,

Fans look on and cameras flash as Kenny is interviewed at the televised TNN Music Awards in Nashville, Tennessee, in 2000.

the country music capital of the world. Fans call it "Music City."

It's All Okay

He found work singing at a bar called the Turf. It was a pretty rough place. Some nights, the audience was mostly poor people who were just trying to stay warm. Kenny remembers, "I played five or six nights a week if I could get it, four hours minimum, for five dollars an hour and tips. When you're making music in Music City, it's all okay."

Then Kenny got a break. A friend shared a tape of Kenny's music with some people in the recording business. That tape got him the chance to audition with the Opryland Music Group. It was a success. He left the audition with a songwriter's contract. Kenny Chesney was on his way to the big time.

Fact File

Kenny remembers the poor people at the Turf. He wrote his will so some of them will receive money.

16

Martin Guitars

Martin acoustic guitars are famous for their beautiful sound. They are very expensive. Kenny bought one because he wanted his music to sound its best. Many famous musicians use these guitars. Bluegrass legend Lester Flatt played a Martin. So did Elvis Presley, Bob Dylan, and Johnny Cash. Rock stars Eric Clapton and Stephen Stills play Martin guitars.

In 1975, Elvis Presley was "The King." When Kenny was six, he got a Presley album. He says, "I listened to that album over and over again. I used to . . . pretend that I was Elvis."

Fact File

The Opryland Music Group is a publishing company. It prints music written by old-time country stars and by new song writers, too. The Group gives its songwriters rooms with music, paper, pianos, and, of course, guitars.

Chapter 4

To Feel Honored

Kenny's songwriting contract led to a recording contract. His first real album, *In My Wildest Dreams*, came out in 1993. One song on it, "The Tin Man" became somewhat popular, but the album did not sell well. Then the recording company closed. But Kenny would not quit. He knew, he says, ". . . that I could write songs and entertain people, even when everyone in Nashville was telling me I couldn't."

He found a new recording company. His second album, *All I Need To Know*, came out in 1995. Two songs on it made the country music Top Ten. Kenny was on his way up again. His 1996 album, *Me*

CMA/ACM

The Country Music Association (CMA) began in 1958. It promotes country music around the world. Its annual Awards program honors top country musicians. A similar group, the Academy of Country Music (ACM), started in 1964. Its members want to share their love of country music. The ACM also holds an annual Awards ceremony.

In 1998, Kenny was named Top New Male Vocalist by the Academy of Country Music. His mom, Karen, stood behind him as he waved the award.

Kenny's music —
and his guitars —
started getting
more electric.
Here he is in 2003,
singing tunes
from his album
*No Shirt,
No Shoes,
No Problems*.

And You, "went gold." That means it sold
more than 500,000 copies. Kenny explains
his success, saying, "I wouldn't give up."
He kept dreaming big dreams and
working hard to make them come true.

A New Look, A New Home
One of the things Kenny worked on was
his body. He was eating too much pizza
and too many cheeseburgers. He had
become pudgy. Kenny began running
and lifting weights. He lost forty pounds

When he began touring, Kenny needed people to help with buses, hotels, and T-shirt sales. He hired three men who had played Little League baseball with him. He says, "I needed a part of home out there. I could trust these guys with my life."

and got a lot stronger. He started wearing sleeveless shirts and tight jeans at concerts. His fans liked the new look.

They liked his new music, too. His 1999 album, *Everywhere We Go*, sold more than two million copies. His 2000 album, *Greatest Hits*, sold more than three million.

Kenny bought a house in Nashville. He vacationed in the U.S. Virgin Islands. He fell in love with the ocean and beaches on the islands. He bought a house there, too. His 2002 album, *No Shirt, No Shoes, No Problems*, had some songs about the slow pace of life in the islands.

In 2003, Kenny went on a national concert tour. He played for huge crowds in every city he visited. He was now a country music

Fact File

Kenny often wears a sea shell necklace from the Virgin Islands. He says, "It's like taking a little piece of this place I love with me everywhere I go."

superstar, but he still felt like a small town kid. Kenny said, ". . . you start to feel honored that all these people spent their summer with you . . . told you how your songs were their life."

Things kept getting better. At the end of 2003, Kenny made a Christmas album. In 2004, he released a new album, *When The Sun Goes Down*. It sold half a million copies in its first week! The album later won a Country Music Association Award. Kenny was named the Country Music Association Entertainer of the Year.

Fact File

The Grigsby Twins are back! Kenny's mom and her sister Sharon sang "Silent Night" with him on his 2003 Christmas album.

The Grand Ole Opry

The Grand Ole Opry is in Nashville. Kenny has performed on its stage many times. *The Opry* began as a live country music radio program. It started in 1925, and is still "on the air." At first, the program was called *Barn Dance*. The show just before *Barn Dance* was classical music. One night the radio announcer said, "For the past hour, we have been listening to music . . . from Grand Opera. Now we will present the '*Grand Ole Opry*.'" The name stuck. Since 1978, the program has been on television as well as radio. *The Opry* is now part of Opryland in Nashville. Opryland has hotels, a shopping mall, restaurants, and lots of country music.

This is the stage of *The Grand Ole Opry* in Nashville. The "barn wall" look at the back of the stage has been part of *The Opry* for years.

Fact File

Even though Kenny Chesney is a millionaire, he always washes his own clothes. He says, "I've done my own laundry ever since I was a little kid."

Chapter 5

Live Those Songs

On the day after Christmas, 2004, a tsunami struck parts of Asia. This huge ocean wave killed thousands of people. Thousands more were made homeless. Soon after, Kenny sang at a concert to raise money for the tsunami victims. There he met an actress named Renée Zellweger. They liked each other right away.

Renée wasn't Kenny's first love. For a long time he dated a nurse named Mandy Weals. But she was working and Kenny was always on the road, traveling to concerts. He says, "We would break up, get back together, then break up again. Three years of that went by, and it exhausted us." They finally broke up for good in 2002.

"You Had Me From Hello"

In 1996, Kenny saw a movie called *Jerry Maguire*. In one scene, Tom Cruise is talking to an actress. He says, "Hello," then tells her how much she means to him. The actress interrupts him and says, "You had me at hello." Kenny really liked that line. He wrote a song about it called "You Had Me From Hello." The actress was Renée Zellweger. Nine years later, Kenny and Renée married.

Renée Zellweger listens to Tom Cruise in a scene from the 1996 movie *Jerry Maguire*.

His relationship with Renée kept building. They stayed in touch with phone calls and e-mail. They had secret dates whenever their schedules allowed. In April 2005, Renée showed up at one of Kenny's concerts. She gave him a kiss onstage. It was their first public appearance together. Just two weeks later, they got married.

Fact File

Are you going driving with Kenny? Mandy Weals was Kenny's girlfriend for many years. She says, "Make sure you always have windshield wiper fluid in your car. He loves a clean windshield. It was a running joke between us."

Barefoot on the Beach

The wedding took place on May 9, on St. John, in the Virgin Islands. Renée wore a long white dress. Kenny wore slacks, a white shirt, and his cowboy hat. After the

Helping a Hospital

St. Jude is a famous hospital in Memphis, Tennessee. It treats children who have cancer or other diseases. For many people, the hospital is free. Poor families never have to pay for treatment at St. Jude. The hospital was founded by an entertainer named Danny Thomas. Today, other entertainers raise money to help keep St. Jude free. Kenny Chesney is one of them. He has given money to St. Jude for many years.

ceremony, they walked barefoot on the beach. Within days, however, Kenny had to go back to his concert tour. Renée had to travel around the world to promote her new movie.

Over the following months, they were with each other for only a few days. Soon, they both knew the marriage was not going to work. Their careers would keep getting in the way. Kenny's marriage to Renée ended after just four months. His music career, however, kept getting better.

Kenny's new album, *The Road and the Radio*, was a huge success. His concerts were drawing thousands of fans. He was named Entertainer of the Year by the Academy of Country Music. The next

Fact File

Kenny's neighbors in Nashville are country singers, too. Tim McGraw and Faith Hill live next door with their three daughters. Kenny likes to spend time with them and swim in their pool. Faith got Kenny to paint his kitchen dark green.

Kenny raises his prize after being named Entertainer of the Year at the 2006 Academy of Country Music (ACM) Awards.

year, 2006, Kenny performed at the White House. He released a live album called *Live Those Songs Again*. He was again named Entertainer of the Year by the Academy of Country Music. He got the same award from the Country Music Association.

Kenny Chesney is at the top, but he never forgets who got him there. He still likes connecting with his fans. He enjoys telling a story about some fans and one of his songs. The tune is about a tractor. Kenny says, "Some kids sent me a video of themselves in tuxedos, going to their prom on a John Deere tractor. Those kids will remember that for the rest of their lives. And they will remember that song, and they will remember me because of it."

Yes, they will. And Kenny will remember them. Connecting with his fans is still what it's all about.

Time Line

1968	Kenneth Arnold Chesney is born on March 26, in Knoxville, Tennessee.
1991	Graduates from East Tennessee State University; moves to Nashville.
1993	Releases his first album, *In My Wildest Dreams*.
1995	His album, *Me And You*, "goes gold," selling more than 500,000 copies.
1997	Named Top New Male Vocalist by the Academy of Country Music.
2003	His song, "The Good Stuff," is the Billboard Country Single of the Year; named Top Male Vocalist by the Academy of Country Music.
2004	Named Entertainer of the Year by the Country Music Association; *When the Sun Goes Down* is named Album of the Year by the Country Music Association.
2005	Marries actress Renée Zellweger; is named Entertainer of the Year by the Academy of Country Music.
2006	Named Entertainer of the Year by the Academy of Country Music.
2007	Wins People's Choice Award as Favorite Male Singer.

Glossary

acoustic (guitar) — an old-style guitar that is not electric and does not need an amplifier.

annual — happening once a year.

audition — a try out or test.

campus — the buildings and land that belong to a college or university.

contract — a written and signed agreement to do something.

Grammy — awards given by the recording industry each year to the top performers in each kind of music.

marketing — finding ways to make goods more attractive to customers.

prom — a fancy dance usually held near the end of high school or college.

promote — to tell about, advertise, or move forward.

tsunami — a huge, fast-moving ocean wave, caused by an underwater earthquake or volcanic eruption.

tuxedo — a very formal suit for men; often worn by the groom at a wedding.

will — a written document that tells what will happen to someone's property and money when they die.

To Find Out More

Books

Grand Ole Opry. Robert K. Krishef (Lerner Publishing Group)

Kenny Chesney. Blue Banner Biography (series).
Michelle Medlock Adams (Mitchell Lane Publishers)

The Long Gone Lonesome History of Country Music.
Bret Bertholf (Little, Brown)

Web Sites

Kenny's Web Site
www.kennychesney.com
Photos and information about Kenny's life, music, and tours

The Country Music Association
www.cmaworld.com
Country music information and lists of Awards

The Academy of Country Music
www.acmcountry.com
Country music videos, news, and lists of Awards

Publisher's note to educators and parents: Our editors have carefully reviewed these Web sites to ensure that they are suitable for children. Many Web sites change frequently, however, and we cannot guarantee that a site's future contents will continue to meet our high standards of quality and educational value. Be advised that children should be closely supervised whenever they access the Internet.

Index

About the Author

William David Thomas lives in Rochester, New York, where he
works with students with special needs. Bill has written software
documentation, magazine articles, training programs, annual reports,
books for children, a few poems, and lots of letters. He likes to go
backpacking and canoeing, play his own Martin guitar, and obsess
about baseball. Bill claims he was once King of Fiji, but gave up the
throne to pursue a career as a relief pitcher. It's not true.